WITHDRAWN

W9-CDM-803

BY NED O'GORMAN

Poetry

1959   *The Night of the Hammer*
1961   *Adam before His Mirror*
1964   *The Buzzard and the Peacock*
1968   *The Harvesters' Vase*

Prose

1969   *Prophetic Voices:*
          Ideas and Words in Revolution
1970   *The Storefront:*
          A Community of Children
          on Madison Avenue and 129th Street
1971   *The Blue Butterfly:*
          A Book for Children

THE FLAG
THE HAWK FLIES

NED O'GORMAN
THE FLAG THE HAWK FLIES

Alfred A. Knopf   New York   1972

PS
3565
G6F5

B29508

ST. PAUL PUBLIC LIBRARY

This is a Borzoi Book published by Alfred A. Knopf, Inc.
Copyright © 1972 by Ned O'Gorman.
All rights reserved under International and Pan-American Copyright Conventions.
Published in the United States by Alfred A. Knopf, Inc., New York,
and simultaneously in Canada by Random House of Canada Limited, Toronto.
Distributed by Random House, Inc., New York.

Library of Congress Cataloging in Publication Data
O'Gorman, Ned, 1929– The flag the hawk flies.
Poems. I. Title. PS3565.G6F5 811'.5'4 72–171145
ISBN 0–394–47317–5

Manufactured in the United States of America
First Edition

"The Drunken Organ Repairman" first appeared in Horizon

To

ILSE POLITZER
CAROLYN GELLAND
MARK VAN DOREN
JORGE GUILLERMO

and to the memory of

SIR HERBERT READ

Contents

3   Color

4   The Horse

7   Ten Poems of a Misanthrope

9   1 *Garlic*

10   2 *Kites*

11   3 *Gold*

12   4 *Bells*

13   5 *Fences*

14   6 *Children*

15   7 *Windows*

16   8 *Flowers*

17   9 *Colors*

18   10 *Water*

19   The Drunken Organ Repairman

21   The Art of Poetry
or What Occurred in a Day—
Block Island

25   Nine Prayers to the Trinity
to be Sung by the Nuns
of Regina Laudis at Matins

28   On Reform

29   Plato

31   The Mud Bird

33   A Philosophy

35   The Metaphysician

36   Bach

37   The Line

38   Sandcastle

39   Joshua,
      the Periwinkles and the Bonfire
      on Heroic Beach

43   The Resurrection Day
      of a Brown Bear

45   A Net of a Poem
      for Ilse Politzer

46   Giotto

49   To Sister Ann
      on the Occasion of Her Being
      a Nun for One Day

50   The Self the Only History

51   Paperweights

52   Genius

53   The Glutton of the Ivory Table
      or Never Say Die

56   The Muses or the Irrelevancies

58   The Limit as It Is Observed
      by Her Lover

59   To a Friend
      Who Once Was Rich
      and Then Was Poor

62 Dan Brick Talks to God's Wife

65 A Memory of the Childhood
    of Jorge Guillermo

67   1   *The Armoire*

68   2   *The Stuffed Dog*

69   3   *The Pillar and the Pilaster*

70   4   *The Bottle of Guerlain*

71   5   *The Baptism*

72 Drunk on the Lord's Wine

73 The Eagle

75 When I Would Love
    and Cannot Love

THE FLAG
THE HAWK FLIES

COLOR

Blue is the stammerer's color.
Yellow, the color of the lion tamer.
Red, the signum of the clown.
White is the flag the hawk flies.
Orange, the kingdom's staff.
Green, the water bug's legs on the bank.
Black is the father's dream.
Rose, the candle-maker's, purple, the jeweler's colors.
Ochre, the potter's wrist.
Lapis, for the seated knight.
Opal, the bear.
Burnt sienna, the plowman's hood.
Cobalt, the color of the horse asleep.

Peridot is the color of the steeple jack.
Olive is the wind over the steeple.
Wasp green, what the steeple jack sees sprout from the timber of his fall.

Dun is what the rain turns over in the grave.
Turquoise, the color of a toad's death.

The garnet is the color of the trumpeter.

The color of blood is no color for in the ground
it turns like a bullet toward the root of wheat
and drives through snakes and seed
to rise up like breath in the simple grass.

THE HORSE

I am the horse that built the way
to the willow grove. Roots kick at
my hoofs. No flower still. I sway
through the corn like a judge.

This day I took him to a hollow.
Early it was. Just dawn. The
mist in the stall around my eyes. A fallow
time to dream the last horror.

He woke me with a slap on my rump.
I neighed the frost down from
my mane. The lump

of salt in my feed box like a
marble step on a holy stair
slides along my tongue. Start a
high day by backing smartly

from the stall. I do. And stand
head licking the air as he
throws tack upon my back. A grand
bit of leather too, shined

like amber, spurs and bit cold
but warmer than my hide pushing
against me with a silver bold-
ness that sends me stamping

on the floor. He led me to the road,
down to Skunk Hollow Lane,
mounted me, drove his heels in. Load
of him on my back and the morning

stirred wildness through me. I laid
out the way to the willow grove
and stopped there in my canter. Made
the morning was: sun up over the

Griggs' barn. Cows moving out to the field
the last day before their winter
hermitage. The dust settled from my

road. The gold oak; the red maple.
A wind from the wood carrying nuts,
frogcalls and logs and mushrooms full
of summer death. He shouted

in my ear. "Look, look, beast, a lake,
a lake there in the hollow. A mile long."
He leapt off. I smiled. No lake. A fakery
of morning. But he ran down to the shore

expecting whales. But there he saw just
a puddle. I'd done it with the morning light.
"Ah," he cried to me, "No lake." The crust
of day broke. He saw it for what it was.

"It seemed to reach to the Griggs' silo
and was large enough to sail upon. Nothing,
nothing but a still pool; a pile of low
weeds and rock in the middle of it.

A beetle and a dead bird on the bank."
He leapt on me and laid his head upon my
mane. I turned and ran him through the blank
morning; he had dreamed it as it was not

and it was now mere space and light. But
I heard it when we turned: how the whale
nudged the rocks away; how the flock
of gulls settled on the bank; how the

freighter moved past the Griggs' silo;
how the sun burned down upon the castaway;
how the eel and shark laid themselves on the pile of low
weeds and rock and turned the willow grove into salt.

TEN POEMS
OF A MISANTHROPE

1

Garlic

This fine world is now too fine for him.
He needs a limitation to his style,
something to deflect his gaze
as he lifts the shade to look upon the grass.
He peels a clove of garlic, jams it between
his teeth, bites down, then lifts the shade
and all the borders steam as if they had been cut by lava.

2

Kites

He cannot stand the law.
He'd followed it and had broken pennies
on the backs of tigers doing it.
He'd be lawless and no man's bird.
He bought a kite, unrolled it,
and a thunder cloud floated up printed on white paper
held to a hexagon by 6 thin slivers of black wood.
He let it go and he exploded like a bulb
on the stone terrace.

3

Gold

It was always in his marrow,
the spoiling of it away there in the dark pastes
of his life. He hacked away at the outside of
his chest where the mine bone lay
and lifted out a nugget of pure yellow stuff.
He called it gold and hitched it to a chain around his neck.
He shuddered like a tower split from a church by an iron ball.

Bells

They rang at the wrong time as if
they were invaders not expected till
tomorrow—the bastions just up,
the mortar wet, the bricks slipping.
He never knew when to feed the tigers.
They were starved at one and the bells began to ring at five.
After a year of nothing the tigers bit a window in their cage.
They got him up a tree and
after a hectic yawn he died
at the thirteenth stroke of noon.

5

Fences

"One there between my heart and the hill."
The workmen built it out of new birch planks
and planted corn and scallions along the base.
He looked at the month come down over the waters.
"June" he said to his wife and they walked the length
of it to the water's edge.
There were shells there he'd never seen before:
"Must be the revolution sent them from the China Sea."
His wife laughed but she did not see the claw shoot out
the yellow one with the green whorls.

6

Children

They played over his head in a cage on the roof.
Their teachers drove them there each morning after the flag
was raised and the bacon fried for them in the kitchen
beneath the stairs. He watched them come up the trap
door and climb the jungle gym and wished the parrots
and monkeys in his dreams would chase them down into
the streets where he'd set the tigers on them. He hated
children and his sons and daughters knew it and sent him
burrs and scorpions in the mail.

7

Windows

Close them.
Open them.
Take the jar of zinnias away.
Put them back.
Draw the shade.
Raise it up.
I'll watch the snow through the membrane of glass
as if I looked at thunder through a veil.
He picked an andiron up and shined it with his sleeve,
then heaved it on the floor;
the glass broke, the snow stampeded and he
heard his bones crack as if a mighty will
had called the void back into paradise.

8

Flowers

Love had just finished him for the last time.
He bought lilies from a vendor in the market
who sat beneath her wide-awake like a submerged hill.
He put them in a silver vase on the mantle
and watched them grow until
they reached the ceiling and turned on him
winding through the wainscot and the rugs
like antelopes and gazelles through the sprint of the cheetah.

9

Colors

I've invented wail, a color that is all colors—
no colors. I've had enough of red and yellow, orange
and green, seen them come and go and now mix
wail from the dredges of the prism. It is brightest
when it falls on the shadows near the fishpond;
the underwater darkness lost in wail drive the goldfish
to the surface where they gleam like torpor.
Wail everywhere I look and delight in it though
now and then as I die I watch the black loam
in the river bed undermine me in my last dreams.

10

Water

I am building a bridge to float me out when the rains come
to float out my neighbors, their rose hedges and their daughter
Belle. We'll go on opposite currents; me to hell,
them to the icebergs. Their ark is ready now; they've moved
in the great Sheraton desk, four Adam fireplaces and one
Sèvres dish. I shall stand on my bridge with nothing but
a mirror and a stone and string; one to see the face I've
grown to hate as it sinks and the other to sound the level
of the earth. Ah, it's begun now and fills the cracks in the windows.
The sound has woken the dogs. They suspect the worst
and gnaw like rats at the door sill where the flood begins to seep.

THE DRUNKEN
ORGAN REPAIRMAN

Easter 1968

When the church was built it was built into it.
My blood into my neck; forehead to scalp;
blow of my heel on the pavement to my elbow;
rise of a hill to the stick pushing to the summit.

On the first Sunday in Lent when the organmaster
pulled the great manual from the oaken bank,
alarms—beetles and spiders falling through iron—
slid down the walls and stirred the flowerets
on the ladies' hats who had come to take pleasure of the Lord.

It had been in the ribs two hundred years.
When a hymnal fell to the floor or a child wailed
when the holy oils slid up its nose, the organ
spat a low hustle through the air. Death drew
a grey wind from the grill and snuffed
the candles stuck into the coffin lid.

He came from Maine, with a satchel of wrenches
and tuning forks, three cases of gin, a camping bed,
two lanterns, a mending torch, a can of oil and broke
it down to the nails and clamps that hold the pipes
and keys to the magnets in the pith; he spilt
oil upon them like a rain god until it seemed
they breathed.
    It took a year to cure the spasm
in the pipes. The smell of gin, oil, fire and gas,
like a motor over a mechanic pit, hung in the nave
until Pentecost when he sprinkled gin in the center

of the pumps and bellows and walked out the Church
toward Maine.

        The organmaster pulled the great manual
from the oaken bank and alarms of the Paraclete—
fields of violets, stone fences, honey bees, wrens
in the barns, crashed against the white buds and
split the green wood in the apple trees.

THE ART OF POETRY
OR WHAT OCCURRED IN A DAY—
BLOCK ISLAND

Is a poem a sign so abstract no fit could
buckle it? I work it like a drudge doing
the last bit of a marble passageway to a con-
clusion.

This path over the field
drones in the tendril
of the sea.
The honeysuckle lifts its silver
eyes to the bees.
In the falcon's dream
the fieldmouse
hides in the fiery shade
of his hungry claws.

Dorothy van Ghent said to me:
"You babble on as if everything
were
a hoot of God.
Breathe in
a preposition
now and then
lest you end up in a whorehouse,
a second-rate Gauguin
in a phony Samoa."

I saw a small red flower
yesterday. If it lay between
the leaves on the stem
of a fern, there'd be light
and place for sky and shadow
to fold in. It is beaded
to the earth by one hairy root:
a small thing, like my will,
my passions,
my tolerance
for clams.

The four corners of my room
are filled with light;
north, east, the southward and western places
blaze
still as the Great Salt Marsh.

The speed of light
and flowers from fields
once heavy with
burned shadows.

At the top of the stairs
the curve of the earth
hums.

———

Mrs. Dupont's jeep
does not disturb the
cygnets in Siah's pond:
the motor is from
an old Rolls Royce.

Her Florentine straw hat
is tied beneath her chin.
She drives to the beach,
settles her wicker chair
into the sand
and opens *Wild Life on Block Island*
to the chapter
"Falcons and Hawks."

The crests of the waves
splinter like scallop shells
cracked by a tremor in the ocean shelf,
each tendril
clear as the gills
of a mesozoic fish
trapped by ice
within a white stone.

"Sacrifice, kites, battle cries,
the shadow of my wicker chair
upon the sand." These she
noted down in her book,

closed it and watched
a falcon lift into the sky,
set his beak into the wind
and pulled it after him
toward the hills
where night-shade
pulsed in the hedges
where the fieldmice slept.

"He brings to his nest
the food of the waves,
like blackberries upon his wings.
He circles above me:
does he think
I carry spiders and beetles
in my fist?"

She opened her hand and a silver watch
shined like a broken bone
into her eyes.

"Ninety-two years now.
All is still the same.
This bird is the con
clusion
of the day."

NINE PRAYERS TO THE TRINITY
TO BE SUNG BY THE NUNS
OF REGINA LAUDIS AT MATINS

God the Creator who made whales
and Jesus our Brother who wept
and ate bread
and the Spirit
who sprung the latch upon this birdsong
listen

God the Father who draws up
the wheat
and Jesus our Brother who
climbed mountains
and the Spirit
the plank they tread
listen

God the Builder of the sun
and Jesus our Brother who slept
through the night
and the Spirit
who thinks on the sea currents
listen

God the Father who halved
the void
into light and dark
and Jesus our Brother
who went to the well for water
and the Spirit who

holds the poles
apart
listen

Father of the bulls' horns
and the ribs of sharks
and Jesus our Brother who loved
deserts
and the Spirit
who plants roots in frost
listen

God the Maker of the wrist
of Bach
and Jesus our Brother who loved
fishnets
and the catch
and the Spirit who hungers
for the clocks
in snails
listen

God the Master who makes
the emerald
savor of the sky
and Jesus our Brother who
bit down on wood
and the Spirit who

grows poppies near marigolds
listen

Father God who lames beggars
and hurts
the widow when she thinks
and Jesus our Brother
who forgives the tides
their burial of corn
and the Spirit who remembers nothing
but the morning
listen

Father who dropped the seeds
into the mud
and let the green bark
dwell with the sloth
in Adam's wood
and Jesus our Brother
a sail upon the waves
and the Spirit
the birdsong
listen

ON REFORM

If they did not live you mean they did
not own a coat or shoe buckle nor answer
to a call: Respicious, Numpha,
Felix of Valois, Bacchus, Symphorosa.
That at night they did not turn down
the sheets and crawl into bed with wife
or child and rise up in the morning
to hear the lions roar in the dens beside
the river. If you name me am I then alive?
If you un-name me do I die and break the
flowerpot set above my tomb? When
the Lord comes to bring me to my bones
from days amidst the unflawed anemones
will I find my master blind to all I died
so gory for and hear him decree me null
and void and never was?

            Do Catherine, knuckled
on her wheel, Christopher, knee deep in mud,
Valentine and his mating birds, Placcid
and Ursula, their followers and their dreams
of Paradise stand alone now in the marble shadows,
their chapels burned, their statues rendered
into forks and spoons? But, I think,
like Aeneas, Hamlet, and Antigone they storm
the earth still, even as they fall, and sing
again, stronger than before, their blooded,
emblazoned, ruined prayers and swerve
closer to the face they felt in the lions' teeth.

PLATO

Plato fished. By birth he was an angler.
His mother said: Cast flies at the world.
She'll bite. He put a beetle in his cap
and set off to the grove of winds
where ivy crept into the air like eyes
and lay against a log.
Upon my neck this log rests well; soft the
lichen. He moved the air with his hand
and wrote upon it: Epotem. Metope.
Between the triglyphs
in a frieze the riddle of the poem.
He cast the line, grinned at the light,
and tied the line to his toe.

A yellow fish bit the lure
and lay upon the grass spending
its blood in the dirt, slapping the earth
as if it were a child kicking against a rock
it stumbled on. "Epotem." He beckoned it.
"Epotem." The lake rolled up toward the sky.
Weeds bent toward the ants gathering round
the yellow fish. The gills barked
for the shore and the eyes slid to the back
of the brain. Signs of priests and comets
burned on the trunks. Plato turned
the fish over in the grass.

Plato thought: the yellow air. The waters.
The shadow of blood. The word seeks
its living waters as roots do, as the snail does.

The grass burned as if the pool had mounted
land and the fish, in its forbearance,
inhabited the upper world like a sail.

THE MUD BIRD

She brushed off the dust that settled on the rolls
of raisins and hazelnuts. She lit the candle
in the window and called her child to supper.
The upper room was ready for the night; she
had folded back the cotton sheets and opened
the green tin box that held the bones from Sinai.
The sun snapped in the top branches of the tamarisk tree.
In the kitchen the porridge thickened in the bowl.
She called her child again to table but he played
in the mud at the end of the street and did not
answer. He'd seen a rose in the morning
and wished to make it fly when the leaves
moved and the thorns cast acid shadows on the bricks
the rose vine climbed upon. He pressed a bird
from the mud and held it in his hands like pollen
drifting on the tongue of a bee. He shattered a speckled
stone and pressed in the fragments where the wings
would be and waves of blood curved over
the earth and ran into the mud. Dead fish
in the oven saw a shoal of claws come up
from the fire. The child pulled the mud out
to the edge of a feather and peered into the breast
and whispered: "You are a bird, fly." It lifted up
its belly from the ground, fluttered its wings,
but could not mount the air. The child looked again
within the bird and said: "Fly, I am Jesus.
Build a nest in the top branches of that tamarisk tree."
The mud bird laid his head in the dust.

His beak curled and black feathers
fell like scorched fans upon the ground.

His mother stood beside the child and said:
"But boy he has no name. You may be God
but it will not hear you if you do not name him."

The boy bent over the void the mud bird
had summoned from the earth (life is terrible
for a creature in the hands of gods) and called out,
"Robin, Robin, Robin." It leapt into the sky and touched
the child with the shadow of its wings
and the last mud from its airy claws.

A PHILOSOPHY

In the world we know one thing
and one thing only: that love
is not easy and likely to trouble dreams,
turn the mind onto droughts
and the end of hope. In this world
we find the one we seek
and then would drive it out
as if it were a fog under the door
threatening the hearth.
It was always so. Penelope
felt the loom warp; the oak
breaks into crimson and the green
sands on the bottom of the turtle pond
suck in the lily. Let it be
so: if a philosopher would find
the sorcery to end all strife
in love, banish him.
If a face, summoned from the mud,
is doric in the brow and if, when the fire
settles in the nostril and the light fits into the space
between the eyes the sound is a
door opening toward a drumming
in the trees, then leave the room
and spend the day away from windows
and mirrors for that loved face
comes again and again and will not
stop coming when you banish it.
This is certain too: you cannot

banish body from the body; that
is what love is at the beginning of love—
the body and just the body. If
you would have it other, leave this world
and live upon a leaf in an Indian sky.
So. There is nothing for us then but love.
It is man's way in life. To love
and then not to love. It is so and it will be
until the end of love; until the body's end.

THE METAPHYSICIAN

The nave of the syllable is uttered. The belltower
echoes the syllable and the clerestory bolts
the syllable to the keystone in the portal where
the virgin and the saints spin through their rigid glory.

The rose windows drift in the moss and vines of the outer walls.

The metaphysician neighs being to the spiders in the apse.

Thus it rings: truth, touched by fire and light;
object in water; orange on a table; child with hoop
at his heel; dust on a silver dish; these objects
in their altitudes and spheres of shadow.

The bulk and heft of its periods: shells, kelp, wooden spools,
pink skeleton of crabs and tracks of sea wren impale the surf;
the word rests on the strand of the text;
ivory ladders of signs, burnished verbs, waterfalls of adjectives,
and the senses nailed to the margins, blue and yellow as eagles and waves.

In the hollow of the hillside, honeycombs and barrels of clover wine
spill in the winds that lie athwart the fields of Silbury in view
of the sacred mound on the Way of Mwnhir where fern and grazing cattle
blacken out the sun. Branches of bees and flowering nuts spin
in the cleft of being where metaphysician utters the syllable:
OPHIR   ENS   AMPHEE   ELI   ARBIME   EUREKA

BACH

The fleur-de-lis and the toad.
The stone held in the hand
beneath a waterfall. A shell lifted
from sand. A flower released from the bee's
wing. The reeled-in kite, heaving on the grass,
hobbled with the brute curve of space.
The grass lit by morning leaves.
The shutters fall back from the kitchen.
The garland of moons that hangs over the salt
and garlic breaks. The bread stands like a rhino
in the pan. The small fish lifted up by the oars;
the bulkhead between the hillside and the elves;
the level of pears and apples in a dish.
The shadowed ground of a snake's head;
defiles, crags, small mountains, iron hairs,
baskets of scale, liquid green shale. . . .
The snow covering a tree trunk, branch, dry bud, nest
and cracked blue egg. The eye up against the wind,
watching the whorl of seed in the vortex where
kingdoms rise from upturned buttresses and roofs.
The bear's head of silver webs matted together
then pricked with a snout.

THE LINE

"A confusion of sculptured episodes" in the phrase.
The halt sound; the ruptured signal from the beginning
to the end of the symbol. The crumbs of the middle
of verbs that chip from the loosed fist. Every eagle
knows the faulted plummet to the hare when the meat
escapes down a hole in the plain. The maharaja
his eyes between the Behemoth's ears sees the cur
crushed beneath his chariot's foot. But the progress
endures—the flight, the blanket threaded with rubies,
the line. If struck with the mind it heaves through
like a tower in the wind or a bell cast too soon in water
will turn upon the hammer. The line suspect, the line
flawed, the line tainted; the monstrance, a pod of the eye.
It, that has no foundation but the word: that old
wreck of a lion lying in wait in the crater feeding on anemones
and sleeping on the gazelle's open belly. That line,
my hellion dream, woke me this morning with "every eagle"
and the day took on the words and the sun too
and "every eagle" became the day hovering over me like a feathered scream.

SANDCASTLE

When the sea comes up out of the deep sands
the sandcastle built with that sand is best.
The walls are firmer, the turrets and moats
stand against the battering of the seasons in the waves.
Build a wall with the sand on shore
and it falls after the sun warms it.
Not so with the deep sands: those are sands
that see no light, no parasol. No gulls' eyes
watch them. The dark sands. The volcanic ones
that never breathe wild rose scent.
The sullen sands.

JOSHUA,
THE PERIWINKLES AND THE BONFIRE
ON HEROIC BEACH

3 of May 1969

Where are we standing when we stand
on the sea's edge,
beneath the blue clay cliffs,
in the shadow of the May sun,
on the rocks
and the sea wrack
near shoals of periwinkle?

Joshua knew.

He gathered kelp.

I'd started a bonfire from cork
and a lobster pot.
Sand and rocks piled
around it
to keep the wind from gouging it
into the sea.

Joshua thought of periwinkles.

I kept my eye on the fire and threw
logs, milk cartons, planks
and husks of crabs
and sea spiders
into the maw of the flame
settling into a gale.

I kept it going all afternoon,
guarding it as hills guard their slopes
that no unguarded
plain would climb and settle it into a valley.

So I watched that fire
that no cool hand of the salted
and mottled sun
could caution it away.

Joshua climbed a blue cliff
and wedged himself into a crack
where spring water
fell toward the sea;
the blue clay touched by water
parts, like honey from a blue hive,
through the sand.

Hector would have burned
brightly here
in a funeral pyre
and a ship carrying the maps of Rome
would have found the way clear
from there
at the foot of the blue clay cliffs.

The center of the bonfire
had grown so hot—

a fist of volcano curds—
but Joshua thought of periwinkles
though he brought me kelp
he thought of periwinkles.

The cliffs leaned toward
the blue sky on
their banks of burned heather.

Joshua slipped through the rocks
and wandered
to the periwinkle shoal,
where he had seen them clinging
to the rocks
submerged in the low water
their shells kissing the foam.

But he could not walk there now,
the sea had risen up and buried
the shoals
in heavy water and spray.

He wept, for periwinkles
had been his rage the day long
not the bonfire
and I could not stop him
as he stood alone and mourned his dead treasure.

He walked back to the cliffs and picked
kelp on the way
but the fire had gone out and I laid
the kelp on a stone
and walked with Joshua up the stairs
in the cliff to the field
atop the beach and looked down into the sea
and upon the beach
over toward the shoals where his periwinkles
lay now caught in the rocks' underwater shadows.

THE RESURRECTION DAY
OF A BROWN BEAR

It was not the same, not precisely,
as it had been, but like enough
to make the resurgence of bulked and battering
flesh a charm. Where he'd been all the years
since the lake caved in and he'd sunk
without a sound to the blooming rockbed
of the arctic he did not wish to think about.
He'd some uneasy thoughts about a window
and a blue field but no dream or memory
of the bear he was and life for him without
the bear in him was not life at all.
He'd been called Arroyo and he'd held the hills
near Compostela in his arms. The hills were
his will. He had leaned on every violet
hay stack and apple and no child or lady, shepherd
or bishop in his frock dared go about the land
until they'd knocked on wood and called his name
three times against the light to banish fear.
He was a princeling, descended from a unicorn
and a polar bear. When he had grown old he traveled
north until the arctic circle moved beneath him.
He spent the days tramping on the ice, kicking over
mounds of ancient snow, frozen butterflies and moths
fell like slivers of Sumerian lintels on the heaving
crown of the world.
                    Now 500 years gone by
he feels the sinew and blood begin to blister
along the bone. The rubble of his dust takes on weight

and fur picks out the lines around his eyes. He is
too large for the fathoms of his grave and soon
his paws, his neck, his hip and belly push aside
the ice and frozen wheats and he stands up full
height beneath the waters that on his resurrection day
grow warm and light as pollen. He rises up. When he
puts his head above the surface of the sea he knows
it all again: the violets, the pilgrims on the way
to Compostela, the wail of the wood cock on his tongue
and the herbs and spells of the hills. And starved
from centuries without flesh and blood he pounces on
a singing carriage of novices and their guardians and gulps
them down as if he'd never touched a living thing before.

A NET OF A POEM
FOR ILSE POLITZER

A tunnel: naked, white, marble: the theatre.
Leptis Magna. Blue. White. White. Salt.
Black oil in the sea like a weed. The killing,
skinning, roasting of a lamb. How it was
killed. How it was skinned. How it was roasted.
Homs. Libya. In an orange tent. Estoril.
A boy in a blue cloak walked out of the desert
and held aloft to me a white egg. Birds flying
and singing in the steel girders. A glowering
green thistle. Libyan shepherdesses wear bright
red and blue trousers and shirts. Their trousers
bellow with winds that touch the top of the sand.
Fleece of sheep daubed yellow and orange. It
marks one flock from another. Alma mater:
her ass to the sun and buzzing on her open spine
the dereliction of the book; pages like wings
of houseflies stuck on the rind of a molding lemon.
Talk of the sun in the desert. Her food which
she took but once in a day consisted of herbs
and pulse. She stood in cold water and recited
the first one hundred psalms. The hairbreaths
that hold thought together like a dayspring in
a garden wall. The Abyssinian lion has a brick
forehead. The mask from the Congo with pigtails
and a half open mouth bites the roots of the tree
that talks. The circle: squared.

GIOTTO

It is terrible to watch
the face unfold from a hood
pulled into the room
by the stuff—heavy, brownsack,
lined with thorn and chaff, hemless,
clasped to the shoulder by
a crystal bolt threaded to the fiber
with wires from the roots
of chill barrows.

And so I was
turned into a stem of thorn
when I looked up and saw
the face of God
brushing away the brownsack
and opening his lips
to say
that the glass rose
lay too abreast
the moon
and the dung pile
in the barnyard
would turn into fire
on All Souls
that the forms in the wood
unicorns
spotted lynx
thrush

butterflies
candled spiders
were his

messengers who would bring
corn to the field
fired by the new dung,
fern
to the glass rose
and then
the hood floated back
across his face
the heavy stuff wrapped
tight around his body
and he stepped off
into the light
blocked up about the hillside
in the density
of light caught in alabaster
where the
candled spider
climbed
into the thicket and arbor
in a countryside
of shepherds, their flocks,
periwinkle,
violets,
earth berries

and the fox
who sucks the rockface
of his pit
and still
will not pounce upon the herd.

TO SISTER ANN
ON THE OCCASION OF HER BEING
A NUN FOR ONE DAY

On the first night, a virgin's eyes, once
set upon by her husband's body
in its holy terror, shift, like
glass in a kaleidoscope and take on
new dwelling places of light.

Now Christ shines through the linen
boards of your wimple in the warm hearth
of your will, true as any buck
his dreams cast off.

                    Like a plate
fallen from a mantle when an earthquake
rocked the keystone you have seen the
beginning of all love, breached
by such an one as he who made the world.

THE SELF
THE ONLY HISTORY

I am cut from lapis lazuli
at a high volcanic candling.
My skull is the shell of a star;
my hands the fin of the sea horse
striding through coral, rose-hacked
by the deep water. My nose is French,
my chest from the peat of Clare.
I shall father children who'll range
the dunes in the wake of the gull's
morning visitation on the sands.

The stallion burrows in the honey of the
barley field and leans his head over
the fence where wild roses mass like
bells tolling fire.

The world I am I build from such things as these.

O gold-buckled, burlaped grandee, this self,
my only history, that creeps, a horned calamity,
toward me.

PAPERWEIGHTS

"Let me be such bulk as those," Boethius thought
in the cobwebs. He had seen them on the mantle
of a prince where the sun had knocked colored seeds
into a crystal hill though the garden there did not
move when the world did, nor die when fields
withered in frost.

        Boethius thought he was pretty free
as a whole. But the bars often seemed to hold off the light;
as the flypaper tricks the fly so the bars lured on the light
and sucked it to its rusty jaws.

        He looked at the stalled
light and dreamed of a paperweight of blue whales
migrating toward the north. "If they could be caught
in a sphere of glass, their spouts like willow trees upholding
the sky, what a prize for the ledge of my window where
the bars clot the light. The dome would store it up
like salt for me to savor in my dreams."

        He lay on
the stones and pulled his hood over his eyes.

Afar, a prince moved in his robes and golden world to
a shelf of paperweights and lifted one of pure crystal
to his lips. Hazarded by jewels and ceremonial horns he
breathed on the crystal, and a blue dot and a branch of water
shot into the sun: whales migrating toward the north
swam into the dream Boethius had of self and self apotheosized.

GENIUS

Genius has his dwelling place on a
plateau of tricked winds,
reverberating cliffs and waters
like a sling. In the air
the gravities lie and the abyss turns
into the field. Genius sits
on a rock. It is impossible
to gauge direction by setting a needle on it.
It rests in a bright smoke of light
and is without weight,
unrelated to mountain range
or lode of mineral. Genius faces
the four winds and stacks the universe
into a construction of fire,
science, architecture, magnitude and
letterings. It strives against
the plateau at the convergence
of the centers of many flowers,
curious booty and the flourishing provender.

THE GLUTTON
OF THE IVORY TABLE
OR NEVER SAY DIE

He ate his last ape
and washed her down
with pearls and stuffed anemones.
He frowned,
picked himself like a brood mare
off a patch of clover
and huffed to the sink
tickled his throat with a feather
and coughed it up:
her tits,
the mangled stem,
the pits,
the tail,
the corrupted sands.

Then back
to a bowl of lemon curd,
five dozen clams in frost,
a milky pigeon neck,
and a girl from the country
whom he fucked
on the Ivory Table
then cut her hair,
mixed it with a cup of nectar
from a withered fern,
frowned
and rolled like a bloated hen
to the sink,

pushed his finger down his throat
and spat out:
the pitted rind,
the salty gullet,
clots of hair,
until the gods' afflatus
tolled within him like a greasy bell;
then,
he inched
to the Ivory Table,
leaned over a dish of nuts and garlic
and sucked them
up, as a
plague sucks out a child's
teeth and lymph,
into a tight belch
and fell
head down
on the Ivory Table
striking twice
its sharp corner,
ripping open
his throat
which
when it had parted to his neck
let out a stream of bullets,
teeth,
pages from a holy book,

a boy's ear,
an alphabet of lighted seed.

The final thing he did,
this glutton of the Ivory Table
was to seize the beaded fillet round his head
and let it down
his throat
to try for one
sublime resurrection
before
the
end
of
it.

THE MUSES
OR
THE IRRELEVANCIES

Not always there.
But rather
some other place:
behind a shelf
or
at the top
of a stair
or
on
a
tip
of
sand
or upon
my soul
at its
darkest
(blackest)
shadow.

I think:
but it must
not
be the way
it was
meant to be
when they touched
the brow

TO A FRIEND
WHO ONCE WAS RICH
AND THEN WAS POOR

And suddenly there was nothing.
The cornucopia, tarts fresh from the oven,
lemon with bourbon, croissants on Limoges,
Nayl, the napkin beside the silver dish,
the finger bowl perched on a Porthault disk
of yellow silk, the long fanged hound
incised on the crude emerald ring; that morning—
a paper cup, muffins in a plastic pan,
Nayl gone off to learn a trade; the day
done for him by his wife.
                            The world gives,
then takes away its gold, its lemons and
the loom. You bark at windows at a world
you cannot see. The sink gives back its slop,
doors creak, rugs, peaches, borders the whole
sublime shebang rot and shades spring up,
pigeons foul the terrace and the marble urchin
draws snails and maggots to its arms. Your wife
forgets the orange and the apple on the bedside
table; she folds the sheets too tight and puts
unshredded cloves of garlic in the Shepherd's Pie.

He sulked into poverty. Friends told him sell
the Sèvres, the icons, his wife's ruby belt
and the golden cockerels but he'd not sell a thing
nor lock the doors.
                    "Poverty is poverty. I'll
not sell one treasure for a grain of wheat. Don't

give a damn. I am poor. I was rich once. I have
no need for anything but what I do not have.
If I sold all that's left I'd have less than what
I had before."

                      Nayl made guns in a cellar
in the bitter world; in an alley near a river
and a heavy fog. He oiled his will.

"Let them take it all, those cripples who cut
the web of my loom. Let them blow my head off in the night."

Nayl pitched his will in the weeds outside
the window where they slept, poachers in their
dirt. He had grown thin and dark like a cheek caved in.

"There's someone in the shadow dear. He moves
when I dust. I saw his ears."
                      "Cheer him on.
Lay bread on our brows at night. He'll eat us."

When they slept he pressed the muzzle of his gun against
the glass and caught them, her head against his arm,
in the punctured frictions of his blood. He pulled
the trigger as the ultimate drop of water pushes
against the dam above the gardens and the schools.
They lay the night fixed to the sheets and walls,

their brains poor as mud glittering like fools gold
when the sun came up.

> Nayl told his friends:
> "They were there.
> But now they're gone.
> They left."

DAN BRICK
TALKS TO GOD'S WIFE

"Hello," she said, as I turned the corner
to Luddy's farm. I pick up garbage there
on Monday afternoons at five; I pick up garbage
all week long but God's wife talked to me
at Luddy's place—the richest folk in town;
their garbage's always interesting, fine boxes
from grand shops, Haifa oranges, Guinean gin,
Indian soaps, radishes and carrots flown in from
Texas, rags from Paris, France, and green bottles with
pure spring water at the bottom. The finest garbage.

        I know.

Garbage is my life.
        "What do you have to tell me
of this world where things move and sing and then
erupt with clay?"
        (God's wife jittered like a water beetle
on the earth; her eyes popping out of her head, fingers
fiddling with the air.)

        All I know about dear lady, is garbage.
Do the gods know garbage dumps. There is one nearby. The smoke
from cigar boxes smells like the steppes of Russia. I am a bit of a
poet Ma'am, got that way from being so close to things, as it were.
The pine trees burn here after Christmas like green meteors falling on sand.

At summer's end the barn is emptied out. The Luddys
go away to Spain to scrape the sun and leave me a pile of junk

to sell. Last year I sold some half-filled sacks of oats
and bought myself a telescope. Come along. Jump into
my truck; we'll drive slow, seeing as who you say you are.
The roads are bad. Just spring mud and rocks. That dark bunch
of sleeping fur in the pine tree near the wood shed at the next
turning is a porcupine. He sits all day, comes down at night
to burrow in the rocks beneath the Edge. We're heading there now."
                        (God's wife
drew a mantle of slashed light about her shoulders.)
                        "We're going to the edge
of what? I think this is a riddle."
                        "My dump. The Edge. I call it
that. The town folk who don't hire me come there to throw garbage in
the fires I keep burning throughout the year."
                        "Eternal fires
here too?"
                (Dan did not laugh. He did not understand.)
                        The porcupine crept
down the tree and followed them. A green patina tinged with coke covered
the air. God's wife's fingers clinked with rings that did not shine but **hummed.**
                Dan said. "I am unmarried and live alone."
                        (She pulled the light down
over her eyes. The porcupine, quills erect, crouched at her feet.)
"Do you believe in God, my husband?"

                                "Look. Those gulls. How
beautiful they seem above the edge, fresh from their watch over
the waves where they wait for white smoke to rise from new garbage.
Then they come in to feast."

(One landed then on a heap of severed
shark and tuna heads.)
"They swoop closer and closer, gliding like
angels, but, God's wife, they are no angels. Pick up the telescope.
Their eyes reflect no light; their wings, brilliant from afar
are grey with the raw blood of rats that gnaw the rot in the thickets."

(God's wife lifted the porcupine into her hands. She kissed it, Dan heard
it purr. A gull eyed his throat. He waved his hands to scare it off.)
"Do you believe in God?"
"I believe in gulls and garbage."
God's wife stepped
into the porcupine and left. A gull picked Dan Brick up with its hob-nailed
beak and dropped him in a wave which bit him when he fell, in half.

Back again,
in her place, God's wife looked up through the sparks at Luddy's fields and saw
roots and snails lurch against the earth.
She picked a burning
feather from her hair
The porcupine slept in
the shadow of her chair.

A MEMORY
OF THE CHILDHOOD
OF JORGE GUILLERMO

1

The Armoire

High on the bright front, near the crest, polished with tincture
of wine and bees-wax, where the wood had sprung
into a bowed wing of oak, a garland of spring flowers
lay in the dark loam of the grain. It stood against
a white wall where a frieze of boys and mules
trekked to market, he imagined, somewhere in the garden
beyond. Now, from the terrace, he watched it
in the mixed light of that morning (there had been
rain and sun ever since the cook had brought him
apples and brown bread for breakfast). It pierced
the room like a nail through ice, floating on the
tassel of a key that hung from the lock in the bottom
drawer, a hard iron key he had never seen anyone turn.
He set down the top he had just begun to spin
and let the blocks stand as they were, a spiraling
castle, and walked across the black and white marble
floor, turned the key and the drawer shot open
as if someone had released a hidden spring within.
He looked down on a pile of fresh pressed linen
and from the edge of an embroidered pillow case
a blue butterfly rose up and scaled the glittering
armoire as a shadow of thorn ascends the knife
that prunes the wild garlic gone berserk through the roses.

2

The Stuffed Dog

His aunt who wore white linen
dressed starched as firm
as communion wafers
read him a passage from El Cid
as he knelt at her knee
with his stuffed dog,
The Brute Fandago, in his hands.
(His Father said: She is as wicked
as they come.) Jorge yawned.
She pushed back her sleeve,
lifted up the dog and dug his jaw
into her arm. She screamed
and he thought he saw blood cast
a hot blush on her brittle cuff.

3

The Pillar and the Pilaster

They held up the room,
one pillar and one pilaster
that came from the gloom
of the morning rain and sun,
striding from shadows,
the shafts gleaming
and small plaster ropes
falling like coils of fern
from the tip of the capital.
The butterfly rested like
a strand of burning hyacinth
above him in the air.
From his place on the terrace
it seemed as if the room
were a tower moving up
or a giant setting torches
of sunlight to the ceilings.

4

The Bottle of Guerlain

It was a trick he could not get the secret of:
how light got into the bottle of scent
that rested on a shelf of painted roses
held to the armoire by two braided ribbons.
A piece of wood, weighed down with ambrosia
rested like an oar of shadow on the bottom.
He tipped it over, the stopper fell out
and the stick rose to the top, the scent
falling over him, head, shoulders and legs.
His mother smelt it when he came to supper.
He said:
        I took the top off and
Mama, it smelt like the garden wall.

5

The Baptism

"The Aunt of ours who is not an Aunt
but my Mother's oldest friend held me
when the Bishop blessed my new body
as it entered into the spirit. She wore
a grey silk, Balenciaga summer dress,
plain cut, short sleeves, high neck
with a panel of lighter grey down the front,
a flat emerald ring and a wide brimmed
white straw hat with a grosgrain ribbon of the
faintest yellow round the crown. She stood
in front of the altar, on either side
a basket of tulips, lilies and fern
embedded in moss. When the Bishop poured
the waters over my head I peed and sent
a yellow streak of my interior life down her dress."

DRUNK
ON THE LORD'S WINE

Such drunkenness! The priest had filled
the chalice to the brim and when he took
a sip and the friends around the table
their delicious portion, the chalice came
to me half full of the Lord's earthy blood.
I drank it down in two gulps. It ran like
buds of wisdom in my throat. I'd not eaten
all the day, till the plate of God's bread,
but for an orange in the morning. Suddenly
the wisdom I had swallowed built a trellis
round my flesh and weighed me down with plow,
shears, trundle and ladder of the harvest.
I swayed in my chair. I stood and sat quickly
down again. The floor had leaned against me.
The window rolled from its frame and closed
round my skull. I was drunk on the Lord in a
bright tide of a sensual spell.
                             Well, there I was
six floors up in the middle of a block I knew but
did not know for I was drunk on the Lord's
blood and such a drunkenness it was.

THE EAGLE

That eagle knew iron distances.
No full traps. Hills cracked
by the newborn ice whipped on
the sun's rim, spelled him. His
feathers turned heavy with the
plummeting earth. At the center
of a curve in the miles of his
desolation, he saw, that morning,
the Norseman walk out of his pelt
hut, hitch up his britches with a
leather belt (the buckle, copper,
two jaws of a stunned deer in flight
joined in blunt shriek at his belly)
and kicked aside a crystal lump
between tracks of a wild shadow,
and snapped his fingers. The eagle
watched from his hot branch.
"Come brotherhood, scatter from
the thickets and gnaw my bones.
O this pelt world and its inky heat."
(Then there was one man and one eagle
in the transparent orb of the world's
brain.) "If there be others, come,
enchant, kill, speak and fall asleep
with me in the darkness of my thigh."
(We infer the desert not from the ant
with the dozen red eyes huddled in
the rift between strokes of wind but
from the drift of the pear tree in

the dark. The desert is everywhere,
most certainly just as fullness comes.)
On its hot branch, weighed down with
the hunger of the plain, the eagle crouched
in the man and man in the eagle, drifting,
above, beneath each other, like flowers
aloft. The eagle descended from branch
to branch until it stood uncertain as a
boat on a barn floor, on the earth.
The world lay about them unconsumed,
like a dish of wine in a beggar's dream.
There was a truce of blood, a strength,
of flesh and a gentleness of light when
that man bent, like a green branch
into a pool, in the eagle's eyes.

WHEN I WOULD LOVE
AND CANNOT LOVE

When I would love and cannot love
then I know the rules of love
that render me complete and still.

In this new age redeemed by love,
I cannot dream of love and not awake
and dream of love again
even as I know that dream will
go when this new age,
redeemed by thunder from the fields, is still.

I am not of this opinion
held by some I love
that love is a fit of nerves
and vanishes, if it is ill begotten
in the world, like thunder into barns
where the fields are sundered
from the rocks. I have this opinion:
love a cubit adds to my depth
and height and cannot go from me.

I have said, once when there seemed
just this exquisite joy
followed by another and then another
that love was this and

nothing other but then I learned
that this love was each day
renewed
as the thunder comes through
the ceiling when the storm is gone.

A Note About the Author

Ned O'Gorman is the director
of the Addie Mae Collins Storefront School in Harlem.

A Note on the Type

_____

This book was set in Monotype Bodoni,
which catches more accurately than most cuttings
the spirit of the original Bodoni type.

The book was composed, printed, and bound
by Kingsport Press, Inc., Kingsport, Tennessee.
Wood engraving by James Grashow.
Typography and binding design by Betty Anderson.

JUN 5 1972 S

PS3565
G6F5

E29508

O'Gorman, Ned, 1929–
    The flag the hawk flies. [1st ed.] New York, Knopf;
[distributed by Random House] 1972.

    xi, 76 p. 22 cm. $4.95

    Poems.

    I. Title.

PS3565.G6F5
ISBN 0–394–47317–5   811′.5′4   72–171145
                                                            MARC
Library of Congress   72 [4]

Please Do Not Remove Card From Pocket

YOUR LIBRARY CARD
may be used at all library agencies. You
are, of course, responsible for all materials
checked out on it. As a courtesy to others
please return materials promptly — before
overdue penalties are imposed.

The SAINT PAUL PUBLIC LIBRARY